HOW TO WIN A LOTTERY BY JUST DOING A JOB

Win Your Work Lottery

By
SUBHO DUTTA

DEDICATION

This book is dedicated to Rahu God and Saturn God and
all other Planets, Gods and Goddesses for the sake
of the ocean of humanity of students.

CONTENTS

ACKNOWLEDGMENTS

I thank my parents who have supported me all throughout in the process of writing this book.

CHAPTER 1
INTRODUCTION

Why Is It Important That You Win Your Work Lottery?

I am sure that you know what a lottery is, what it means to you if you win a lottery and that you understand how your life is going to change as a result of that.

I know that the very thought of winning a lottery is going to make you feel extremely happy and I also know that if you actually play and get to win a lottery it's going to make you feel as if all your life's problems and hardships are going to end almost overnight.

You do not have to work again to pay all your bills and you could spend all your time the way you want.

For you winning the lottery would definitely mean financial freedom where you could retire rich and wealthy.

I know, for you, winning a lottery is more attractive as the money you get from that is free and the only cost of getting it is the price that you pay to buy that lottery ticket.

This is certainly a better deal than going to a job and working hard for that paycheck or getting involved in the headaches of running a business to make profits. Right?

Wrong!

Let me here tell you one of the biggest facts and truth.

Getting rich and living a comfortable life by winning a lottery is one of the biggest myths that is being promoted in our society especially for the middle class and the working class.

The thought of winning a lottery is a way and means to escape from reality. The reality of work, of going to an office and working in a job which you probably do not like doing.

Why do we so much fear work or avoid doing our work?

Maybe the work environment is not suitable for you, maybe the pay or the salary is not good, maybe you do not like your boss or your co-workers or there can be any number of reasons for you not liking your job.

It's a real epidemic that prevails where you probably hate your job or you are stuck in your job or you hate going to the office on Mondays to Thursdays and look forward to Fridays so that you can enjoy your weekend.

It's a real drudgery where you might think that the job is not right for you and you are probably not supposed to be there working in the job in the first place.

You might be looking for a job change in order to find a better job or your dream job or you might be thinking about starting your own business.

This is the daily struggle and the pain that you want to come out of to end your daily grind and so deep down you crave and wish if you can win a lottery so that it could solve all your money problems once and for all.

But then we all know the actual reality of winning a lottery.

Statistics clearly show that only one person wins a lottery among a million people.

The lottery is, in fact, a big business where the chances of winning are almost negligible for an individual like you and me but the business which organizes the lottery actually makes all the money.

So, winning a lottery is a very rare phenomenon, and even if you win a lottery of say 100 million dollars do you think you'll be happy and that all your life's problems are going to be solved?

Let me give you a small example to illustrate what I mean by this.

I have seen many people who retire from the government with a hefty lifelong monthly pension without having to work again for money.

It is ok with them for a couple of years but their life is soon filled with a vacuum with no direction and purpose. Their idle and free time eats them away. They have the money but they have got bored and disillusioned with their lives.

You certainly want a better life if you win a lottery.

But the fact is that it is not the case in actual reality as I will explain later how work itself has become the new retirement.

So now you are in a situation where you have a job but you are not satisfied with the work that you do because you think that the job is not suitable for you. Or you are unemployed or you have recently lost your job with no work at all and you probably do not have your own family business or any other strong financial support to make a decent living and pay all your bills.

The structure looks somewhat like this -

Job Dissatisfaction - No Job Or No Work - Unemployed - No Business - No Assets - No Stable Source of Income

On top of that you now already know the reality of winning a lottery or the chances that you have of winning an actual lottery after you buy a lottery ticket.

To make matters worse in this economic reality you have things like big lottery scams and frauds which you receive in your mailbox and text messages.

So what is the solution to your economic and financial reality?

My answer to this is to win your own "Work Lottery".

If you are currently working in a job then you might have heard the terms like a job change or career change, career growth or job growth, career development, career progression, job options or career options, job promotion, career transition, or career pathing or even things like getting a suitable job or getting a dream job, etc...

What do these terms actually mean to you? Do they indicate the complete truth? What is it that you really want?

I think you actually need a Work Lottery.

Winning a lottery is just going to give you a ton of money, that's it and nothing else.

But a work lottery is going to provide you much more than just the money.

Of course, your work lottery is going to definitely provide you with the much-needed money but is also going to provide you with work, a job or employment, a business, a life and a career with fulfillment, a sense of achievement, satisfaction, happiness, a direction, a suitable lifestyle and it's going to meet your life's ultimate objectives, goals, and purpose.

On top of that, your work lottery also has the greatest potential to make you rich and wealthy as well, purely in financial terms.

And the best part is that the chances of winning your work lottery are 100% guaranteed as each one of us can win our own work lottery unlike winning just a lottery which in most cases has almost zero percent chances of winning.

Another good thing about winning your work lottery is that it is free of cost.

You do not have to pay a single dime to win your work lottery which I will explain more later in this book.

If your situation right now is a feeling of dissatisfaction from your current job or you feel that it is a necessary evil to go and work in a job so that you can pay all your bills or it is just that you want a better job and later on want to start your own business or you want to do both a job and a business at the same time starting from scratch or you do not have a job currently and you are looking for work or planning to start a new career or simply you want to get rich and wealthy and live a healthy and rich lifestyle then it is time for you to win your own work lottery.

In the rest of this book now I am going to explain in detail what this work lottery is all about.

What does it constitute and how you can follow my step-by-step process flowchart to activate your own work lottery.

I am also going to point out the mistakes that you should avoid while following this guideline.

So let's get into the meat of the content right away.

Read on!

CHAPTER 2
YOUR LOTTERY TICKET
- HOW DOES IT LOOK LIKE?

Market Demands, Market Needs, and Market Requirements Matching With Your Own Personal Boundary!

For your own work lottery to get activated, there are broadly two main things that are required as shown in Figure - 1.

They are namely -

A. Market

B. Your Own Personal Boundary

Let me now explain the two in detail.

A) The Market - The market represents the demand. In other words, the market is the buyer of products and services.

Figure - 1

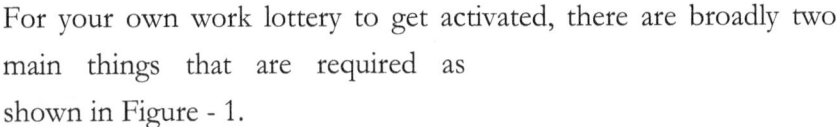

As you might be already familiar with the terms like - market demand, market need or market requirements, or even niches.

It means that there is some kind or type of need in the market for work, solution, product, or service that is required to be fulfilled but is currently unmet.

Now, what does market mean here?

The market here is your boss, your employer, or a company or a business represented by the management who require work.

It also means your customers, your clients, or any particular niche that all require some kind of product or service.

B) Your Own Personal Boundary - Personal boundary represents the supply. In other words, you and your personal boundary is the seller of products and services. It's about You.

Your own personal boundary can be considered like a country or a nation of which you are the government or the administration. You are the president of your own country.

You own this country of yours and you are solely responsible for your country's growth development and expansion.

You have got to see that your personal boundary or your own country is in the sound economic health and is moving towards prosperity.

This personal boundary of yours or your individual country is doing all the economic activities in the form of a job and/or a business to produce the goods, products, and services as required by the market.

Other than the economic activities your own personal boundary has related social activities as well to keep your country happy and productive.

All the economic and social activities should be carried on with utmost secrecy and protection from the outside world.

Nobody should actually come to know what activities you are conducting inside your country (personal boundary) and how you are conducting them.

So be very careful and cautious towards whom you are allowing inside your personal boundary.

You need to, therefore, grant visas to only those people inside your country that you think and consider as favorable, helpful, and supportive to the growth and development of your own country to carry out your economic activities peacefully, productively, and without any hindrance, obstacles, troubles, and danger.

I will explain more on this later in your support system chapter.

The primary objective or purpose of your personal boundary or your country is to produce the goods or services and supply them to meet the specific demand of your market.

So it is basic economics that is involved in your work lottery which is demand and supply.

The point to be noted here is that you through your own country or personal boundary are meeting some specific need or demand of the market which you are only capable of meeting and good at supplying or delivering.

So, there is no competition. Here you are only competing with your own self to better your own country or your own personal boundary.

This personal boundary of yours is a very well-coordinated and well-greased system, a machine, an organism, and your country.

Your Work Lottery Ticket

Market Demand

Supply From Personal Boundary

Passion

Knowledge

Goals

Talents

Skills

Abilities

Efforts

Support System

Results & Scores

Systems & Automation

Results & Scores

Assets

Health, Wealth & Prosperity

Figure - 2 shows the complete process flow chart of this system and its parts which if followed correctly will always give you the right and the best results in your career.

This is your complete work lottery.

There are a few steps or phases by which this system passes through to appropriately meet the demands of the market.

This system of your personal boundary can be broadly broken down into two phases.

The first phase is your job or employment/self-employment phase which is also termed as the Resource Market.

You can consider this phase as your School and College of Capitalism where your primary purpose is to earn your money by doing a job and then pass out from your school and then graduate from your college with a degree.

Importantly this phase is also meant for your studies, planning, and for setting up your own startup business as part of your passion project in this school and college.

So the business that you start and earn from becomes your college degree.

The second phase can be termed as your University of Capitalism where your primary focus would be to grow and scale up your business which you would have already started in your School or College of Capitalism.

This can also be termed as the Product Market.

You can also continue doing any kind of suitable employment or self-employment as well in your university during this phase but that would be your secondary focus

This phase is also important not only for earning your university degree by profitably running and operating your business but is also the phase of your expansions, contributions, and for the fulfillment of your ultimate desires and wishes in life.

Let's now zoom in and see how this whole thing works.

We are going to see now how you are going to achieve this fully activated work lottery.

What are the various processes involved in each phase of this system and what are the actions that you will need to take for you to win your work lottery

So continue reading!

CHAPTER 3
YOUR LOTTERY TICKET - HOW TO ACTIVATE IT?

Playing And Winning Your Work Lottery By Doing Your Job As An Employee Or As A Self-Employee!

———————— ❖❖❖ ————————

We have by now seen how your work lottery looks like, what all it contains, and how it is structured.

You might have got an idea that there is a proper flow in this system and hence I am now going to explain this process flowchart in detail so that you get the best results out of your career and life.

As I have already mentioned that your work lottery gets activated in reality by the simple equation of demand and supply.

The demand is your market and the supply is your personal boundary.

I am now going to discuss how you can activate the first phase of your work lottery here.

This is the most basic and the most essential part of the entire system especially if you are just starting in your job or career after your formal school, college, or professional degree and education.

This is also the most basic and the most essential part if you are unemployed or out of work or just looking for a better job or your dream job and simultaneously you have a strong interest and an inclination towards starting your own business but have no money to invest.

So let's get started!

The market as you already know by now is the demand or the need or the requirement for work or a product or a solution that is unmet and needs to be filled or helped with.

For you the market signifies opportunities!

There are two kinds of opportunities that are relevant to you to win your work lottery.

They are job or employment opportunities and there are business opportunities.

If you have no money to invest and also feel that you have inadequate knowledge, expertise, connections, confidence, and experience to start a business then always start tapping the job market or the job opportunities first.

I need to let you know here that there are many forms, types, and kinds of job opportunities or job markets.

There are good job markets and there are bad job markets.

You can be an employee of a big corporate organization or a medium-size company or employee of a small private firm or company.

You can be a full-time employee or a part-time employee.

Then there are contractual employment and freelance jobs.

You can work by going to an office or you can do a work from home kind of job.

There is employment and there is self-employment.

Self-employment is also a job opportunity only but here you are the boss in your own job and you decide how you can serve your clients by working on your own terms.

Then there are jobs which require you to work even night shifts as in a 24/7 work environment with no fixed offs. There can also be rotational shifts in some jobs.

So you see that there are so many options that you can choose from.

How do you know which one is your greatest opportunity?

Here comes the first phase of your personal boundary in conjunction with the market as illustrated in Figure - 2.

The market produces these job opportunities for you as detailed above.

Each job opportunity is like a lottery ticket in the market.

This lottery ticket has a job description written on it with other details like the company name and company description.

Some of these lottery tickets also mention the value or the amount that this ticket holds which you will get if you win it in the form of a monthly or annual salary or hourly or project or task-based pay.

This ticket also provides details about the exact requirement of the job along with the qualifications and experience required to do the job.

So this lottery ticket in the market in the form of a job notification gives you a fair idea about what that job entails.

There are probably millions of lottery tickets available in the market.

You can go through and see as many lottery tickets in the market as possible in order to buy them.

Now how do you buy these lottery tickets?

Of course, you do not buy them by paying money but by applying to these job notifications and job opportunities by filling out an application form along with attaching your resume and a cover letter.

So the entire process of buying a lottery ticket which you would like to buy is by applying to that job with your resume and a cover letter. Then if it deems fit for the employer you may be offered the job or you may be invited to take a written examination and/or a verbal examination in the form of an interview or a combination of both.

An important question would be that once you get the lottery (I mean the job) how do you know that you have actually won your work lottery?

So, let's analyze your personal boundary now to understand this.

As you can see in Figure - 2, the first phase of your personal boundary constitutes namely your -

Passion; Knowledge; Goals; Talents; Skills; Abilities and Efforts

Always and I say again always keep these seven parts of your personal boundary in the forefront as your only criteria in choosing and buying your lottery tickets from the market.

However, there are two traps that you need to be aware of while choosing your lottery tickets or jobs from the market.

I advise you strongly not to fall into these two traps because if you follow them then they will only disappoint you later.

The first trap is to never give any kind of money to get a job or employment in the form of service charges or fees or medical tests or whatever.

You are not supposed to pay any money to get a job or employment. It entirely beats the purpose of getting or seeking employment and it is a clear chance of getting duped of your money in a scam or fraud.

Also, in certain cases especially in online jobs, you may not be asked to pay any money for a job but you may be asked to click on some suspicious links for a job which might look very easy for you to do with a promise of very high pay.

Don't ever click on such links which might look tempting to you but at the same time can destroy your personal data on your Smartphone and your computer.

There can be instances of hacking in such cases where you might lose money by unintentionally giving away your bank details and other sensitive financial data.

So stay away from such lottery tickets or employment opportunities in the market.

The second trap is to never look at the salary offered in a job as the primary or the sole criteria to get that job. If you do so then you can be in for a great disappointment even if you get that particular job.

I know you do get tempted to apply for a job if that job is offering you very attractive pay or salary. But never fall into that trap as it does not guarantee that you will win your work lottery.

But at the same time if the salary offered is too low that you are disappointed and demotivated then also do not proceed further to buy that lottery ticket as after all it does matter as to how much you put into your pocket from a job to pay all your bills.

You should always take stock of your passions, knowledge, interests, talents, skills, and efforts in choosing your job or your work lottery in the first place.

Of course, there is the score and result component in your personal boundary as shown in Figure - 2 but that I will discuss in detail in a later chapter.

So now let's analyze your passions, knowledge, interests, talents, skills, abilities, and your efforts which are the most important parts in your personal boundary that actually ignites or activates your work lottery

Passions, Knowledge, Interests, and Goals -

When you search and see a job opportunity or a lottery ticket in the market, first see and feel for yourself if you have the passion, knowledge, and interest to do that job as defined in the job application.

Analyze all the information that is provided in the job application with regard to the position, requirements, qualifications, working hours, paid leaves and number of offs, pay or salary offered, and most importantly look at the detailed job description given.

See if you are happy imagining working in that job.

Does that job opportunity provide you with joy and enthusiasm and a life that you can look forward to?

Passion is the energy that you have. Do a little introspection as to whether the job gives you the required energy.

This energy can come to you due to various reasons.

It can be there because you think that the job is available in a good, big and financially stable company and that the company is committed to giving you a salary which you will like along with other benefits.

This joy, energy, or passion can also come to you if the job is a work from home opportunity where you feel that you will be far happier and productive working from home peacefully and at the same time can take care of your family.

This can also be like a freelance or a self-employed independent contractual job opportunity where you give more importance to your freedom and flexibility of when and from where to work from.

If you have been working in an organization where you have trouble with your bosses and management and you feel stuck then this freelance or a self-employed independent contractual job opportunity can provide you with the necessary joy, passion, or energy.

This joy and energy or passion can also come to you if the job is in your subject area or your field of interest which you already know about and have done your studies on and find your subject interesting. You also feel that you are knowledgeable and confident to handle this job without any problems.

This joy, energy, or passion in a job can also be there if you feel that a job can give you long-term career growth and development.

The joy, energy, or passion can also come to you if you think that the job is going to fulfill your life goals and purpose which can be anything and which only you know best.

For example, does the job give you enough pay so that you can manage a family and pay all your bills or for buying a house or a car or to fund your marriage and retirement or it can also be money required to meet medical and other health-related expenses?

Does the job itself give you enough learning opportunity and training so that you can grow and stay in that job for a longer time?

Does the job give you enough time to learn, study and practice setting up a part-time business so that when you decide to leave this job you have enough money, resources, knowledge, contacts, and confidence to reap the benefits of independently starting your own business?

It can also be that you feel that the experience that you are going to gain in the job is directly going to help you set up and start your own business later.

So, you see, that the goals and purpose of entering into an employment or job can be any of your own personal reasons which in turn is going to give you the required joy, energy or passion in doing that job.

Talents, Skills, Abilities, and Efforts -

The second most important aspect of choosing the right lottery ticket or job opportunity to win your work lottery is your talents, skills, abilities, and efforts.

Talents and skills are your tools available only to you to do a particular job.

Talent is your inborn natural tool, whereas skills are your learned or acquired tools in doing a particular job.

If passion is your joy and energy, then talents are your tools and flow that you have in doing a particular job or task.

How much flow you have in a job is determined by your natural ability to do a job exceptionally well and that you are naturally good at doing that job and you find yourself as the best at doing that job more than anybody else.

Talent is your tool that you are born with to do a particular task or job.

If you find a flow in your job then you are certainly at an advantage.

Because you are doing a job that you are naturally good at doing and so it will bring about a work output effortlessly on your part.

Hard work then becomes play for you.

It will certainly make you feel as if you are not working on your job but you are playing in your job. And play as you all know is always fun and brings about immense happiness.

If you take up a job or employment where you do work which you find easy to do not because the job is actually easy but because your innate ability or your own talent makes the job easy and interesting to you then you will never know when the hours pass by in doing your work in that job.

This will result in higher productivity on your part and most importantly you will enjoy doing that job.

You will look forward to each of your working days with happiness and I am sure you will get up in the morning from your bed highly motivated.

Now, the only problem that you may encounter in getting the flow in your job by working as per your talents and skills is that it is not always possible for you to know in advance whether you will get that flow in your job until and unless you start working in that job.

This is the reason why many people change jobs or even an entire industry after complaining about their existing bosses, management, and the company.

So to mitigate this risk and to know if you will have a flow in your job that you intend to join, please make sure to read and understand the job requirements, your role in the job, and the nature of your day-to-day duties that are mentioned in the job offer.

If you are still not sure then please ask questions to your potential employer at the time of your interview about their basic expectations from you and about their performance criteria.

Many times you will come to know or get an idea about the flow in your job at the time when you are asked to take a qualifying test or exam before you are on-boarded in that job.

Otherwise, please work with your boss or your client constantly, have regular meetings with them, and discuss your performance during the periodic review meetings.

Remember, that your boss or your employer, or the management is your client who puts money in your pocket for the useful work that you do for them.

Getting the energy and flow in your job is not easy to recognize.

How can you be sure that the job that you start doing is actually meant for you as per your passions and talents?

In fact, how can you identify that a lottery ticket or a job opportunity that is available in the market is going to be your work lottery?

My answer to this is that it is complex and there is a process of trial and error that you need to follow over a while.

As there are so many lottery tickets that are available in the market, keep buying as many as you like over a period of time.

Then have patience as one of them will surely be your work lottery or near to it.

In other words, keep applying to the jobs in the market and go for your interviews and give your written tests and qualifying examinations.

This is for your own good as it will allow you to assess your own self and find for yourself the best and the most suitable job which only you can feel and know that yes, you have now won your work lottery.

While you are following this entire process of buying your lottery tickets, keep in mind that at no cost ever show your weakness, neediness, hunger, desperation, and helplessness to get a particular job to your employer as it will severely harm you.

Showing such emotions in the form of impulsive behavior in front of your potential employer generally gives an impression that you are a weak person which can severely affect you negatively as you may not get that job ultimately.

Even if you manage to get a job out of desperation and scarcity, your employer might exploit you in such cases.

I understand this situation when you have no job or employment or money or you have recently lost your job or employment or money and you are desperately searching and looking for a job. There are this fear, pain, anxiety, uncertainty, and crisis in such situations.

What is required in dealing with such situations is to build, keep and maintain your emotional strength and balance during this period as you must know that such periods do come in life but they are temporary and soon pass away.

Do not just give away your powers to your potential employer, otherwise, it will be very difficult for you to survive and negotiate in your job.

While negotiating with your employer in a job interview do not put and show all your cards on the table. Keep your powers to yourself no matter how adverse your situation might be.

Why show your neediness, desperation, impulsiveness, and obsession about getting a particular job when there are millions of lottery tickets (job opportunities) available and waiting for you in the market.

Your job is to keep on buying your lottery tickets and instead show your interest, enthusiasm, and patience for a job that you are applying for to your potential employer to get your ultimate work lottery.

While doing so get used to the fear and anxiety that builds up at the time of searching for jobs and at the time when you actually give your job interviews and written tests to get the job. This is normal as each job opportunity does bring in fear and anxiety.

Coming back to your passions, what do you do if you do not know or you are not sure what your passions are, or what you are actually passionate about?

Please follow the below guidelines to know your passions which can help to give you the required energy and motivation to pursue a particular profession, industry, work, job, or employment of any kind.

1. Ask yourself what kind of topics or subjects or areas or fields of knowledge you are deeply interested in and think about a lot in your heart and mind?

2. What are your most dominant thoughts concerning your job, career, and business?

3. What are you especially curious about? What kind of topics or subjects or fields of knowledge do you gravitate towards most?

4. What kind of topics, subjects, fields, or areas you read books magazines, and articles the most and that you are thoroughly engrossed reading them for hours without getting bored?

5. Which are the topics, subjects, fields, or areas of knowledge that you like talking, discussing, and sharing with your friends and family members which truly lights you up and excites you? What kind of subjects fascinate you in a conversation so much that you want to hang around and listen to it?

6. What kind of topics, subjects, fields, or areas of knowledge you are ready to pay money for to attend a seminar, workshop, or training course on?

You can do these six exercises to identify your passions or energy.

Similarly to know your talents or your innate abilities follow the below guidelines which can help to give you the required tools and flow to do your job or tasks in the most efficient, happy, and productive manner.

1. What are some things you are frequently complimented on and praised for doing?

2. Point blank ask yourself what you have always thought you are good at doing?

3. What activities do you engage in that bring you the most satisfaction?

4. What kind of things were you told you do better than others that come easily to you?

5. When did you achieve results that exceeded your and other's expectations?

6. What are some things you have done that have made you feel proud?

7. Ask your friends or people who have been associated with you about what they think your talents are and write and create an inventory of all of them.

8. What do you most enjoy doing for others?

9. On what productive task do you spend a lot of time while enjoying the process?

You should by now have a good hold about your understanding of what your passions and talents are.

But what if you are still not sure or still do not know what your passions and talents are, then don't worry.

I have another far more authentic and scientific solution for this and that is to take the help of meta and hidden science.

Consult a trusted and knowledgeable palmist and an astrologer who I am sure is going to tell you as to where you are trending at, which field of work you are born or destined to do as per your planetary positions on your birth chart and other divisional charts of your horoscope.

They can analyze your hand/palm and your horoscope to guide you, show you and let you know which is the most suitable work that you can do and in which field or area or career path you can not only gain money and wealth but also you will enjoy your work and that too doing it with ease.

I have now covered a lot of ground on the two most important components of your personal boundary.

Yes, they are your passions, knowledge, goals, and your talents, skills, abilities, and your efforts.

If you can get these two parts of your system correct in this first and initial phase then the rest of all the other components will be easy for you to follow inside your personal boundary to win your complete work lottery.

I am now going to share with you the next most vital component for winning your work lottery which is going to give you the highest possible leverage and a tremendous amount of boost into the functioning of your personal boundary as a system and as an organism.

So please continue reading!

CHAPTER 4
YOUR SUPPORT SYSTEM!

*A Vital Component Of Your Personal Boundary For
You To Win Your Work Lottery!*

There is one basic rule that you should always keep in mind and that is "Success Depends on the Support of Others".

In Chapter 3, I talked about you as an individual and stressed the fact that you should always take up any work, job, or employment based on your strengths, unique abilities, and your area of genius.

Yes, your passions and your talents determine them.

But do you think you can work in isolation as an individual and be successful in meeting your goals no matter how much of an introverted you are?

The answer to that question is definitely a big NO.

Your personal boundary is like a country where you are the government and the president of your own country.

So there will be other people in your country living with you, interacting with you, working with you, cooperating with you, collaborating with you, and supporting you as a seller, a supplier, and a producer of goods and services, although, you are still the leader and authority of your country.

In order for you to win your work lottery, it, therefore, becomes important for you to judge and remain careful as to whom you allow and whom you don't allow inside your personal boundary.

This is you, your own personal boundary and you as a country that has its own resources and possesses all the other secret treasures which any country would have.

So don't you think you have to protect and guard your own country so that it is not plundered, exploited, and looted by other people.

You would always want that your country (that is your personal boundary) has a strong productive and prosperous economy with a happy and satisfying social life.

As you are aware that every country issues visas for allowing foreign people inside their country.

There are work or employment visas, tourist visas, permanent resident visas, temporary visas, student visas, investor visas, finance visas, professional visas, religious worker visas, and so on and so forth.

Similarly, you should be careful in issuing visas to people to come inside your personal boundary by deciding whom to give visas to and how much access you give, and what type of access you want to give.

Below is a list of some of the people whom you would like to have inside your personal boundary by deciding to grant them the type and/or duration of a visa.

1. Your personal friends (your social circle)

2. Your professional friends and colleagues (your co-workers)

3. Your spouse and kids (your family)

4. Your parents, brothers, and sisters (your family)

5. Your professional and business contacts (your professional network)

6. Your boss, manager, clients, customers, employer, and the management

7. Your teachers, coaches, mentors, trainers, and religious and spiritual leaders

8. Your team members, employees, maids, and servants

9. Your mastermind

10. Your doctors, lawyers, accountants, financial advisors, tax consultants (your other professional helpers)

11. Your business partners and investors

You can keep on adding further to this list who you think can be a part of your support system inside your personal boundary.

For you to win your work lottery it is very important for you to strictly not grant any visas to the following people inside your country (your personal boundary).

If you have already done so then please make ways and means to deport them for violations of the laws of your personal boundary.

1. People who most of the time show second-class behavior to you. Do not just accept second-class behavior from anyone.

2. People who have cheated you or are cheating you or you think will cheat and betray you.

3. People who mislead you or give you false information. Their advice and information have landed you in trouble for most of the time.

4. People who ask for money from you by misleading you.

5. People who quarrel with you and almost go into fights with you most of the time even though you think that they do good things for you sometimes. Such people are not healthy for you in the long run.

6. People who ridicule you, put you down, or are so negative with you in the conversations that they make you feel inferior most of the time.

Such people cannot in any way be part of your support system inside your personal boundary.

Just do not allow them to get inside your country (your personal boundary) and spoil your country and the work that you do inside it.

The people who are listed as part of your support system are actually meant to uplift you in every situation and make you successful.

They are the ones who will support you, help you, encourage you, and stand by you even if your work, job, or business fails.

The people listed as part of your support system can be both paid and unpaid.

Like for example, you are most unlikely to pay any money to have your parents or your dear friends in your support system.

Whereas you are most likely to pay money in the form of some charges or fees to your teachers, mentors, doctors, or for seeking any other professional help.

But they are still a part of your support system as long as they support you, help you, uplift you, and also serve any of your life and work problems.

You can see as in Figure - 2 that this support system is linked to you as an individual in the form of a cycle and as part of a process flow.

You as an individual are connected to a process wherein you are doing your job, work, or giving service to the market based upon your individual passions, knowledge, interests, goals, talents, skills, abilities, and individual efforts.

Your support system here is mainly supporting, stimulating, and protecting this individual process of yours.

It is acting as leverage, a catalyst so that you can work without any problems and with high energy and productivity.

This support system also ensures that you are not alone, isolated and that your life is happy and peaceful and all your needs are met through them.

Of course, it is a give-and-take relationship as all human relationships are based upon exchange.

I mean you also need to give your time, money, value, and attention to your support system so that you receive their help and support.

You should also remain aware here that the market from where you receive your work, job, or employment can comprise your boss, employer, management, clients, or customers who in turn also become a part of your support system as this process flows on.

If you allow your boss, your manager, your team leader, your clients, or the management inside your country (personal boundary) then you should be granting them a work visa or a professional visa or even a business visa as you are going to have a working relationship with them.

So build your support system with care and utmost attention.

Nurture it well as this is one of the most important and vital components in your entire system of a well-oiled machine.

This is one of the biggest investments that you can make for yourself and you do not have to pay money all the time for building your support system.

The quality and the standard of your support system will be determined by your individuality and your thinking and attitudes towards your individual passions, interests, knowledge, goals, talents skills, and abilities, and your efforts in seeking and doing your work, service, job or employment from the market.

This support system is for you and is going to remain with you throughout your life for the purpose of doing your job and for running or growing your business later on in the next phase of your personal boundary.

So benefit from it by allowing the right people inside your personal country or your personal boundary.

You can see in Figure - 2 that this support system is also connected to your results and scores and the systems and automation component of your personal boundary like a cycle and as part of the process flow chart which I am going to discuss in detail in the coming chapters.

You might be wondering by now that I am again and again telling you how to win your work lottery but I have not talked anything about money.

How are you going to be rich and financially wealthy?

After all, winning the lottery does mean that you are going to get a lot of money. Right?

Yes, I am going to cover that right away.

So read on!

CHAPTER 5
YOUR RESULTS AND SCORES!

Graduate From Your College By Doing Your Job To Earn
Your College Degree With A Business Start-Up!

I am now going to discuss the last component of the final phase of your work lottery and that is your results and scores.

I have now discussed with you the entire process that is involved in the first phase for you to win your work lottery.

Below is the equation that I want to stress upon you which is -

Process = Score

I am sure that you must have attended some sort of a school, college or an educational institution where you have studied and got your basic education and qualifications.

Otherwise, you would not have been able to read and understand what I am talking about in this book.

So what happens in a school or a college?

Yes, you study your subjects which you choose, taught and helped by your teachers and your private tutors or coaches and at the end of a semester or the end of a month or a year, you are allowed to sit in an examination or test which you need to clear and pass hopefully with good results and scores.

Let me explain to you what is happening here by taking the example of a college.

You take admission to a college with a definite purpose, mission, and goal regarding your career, field, and profession.

You choose your own subjects or area of study that you want to pursue because you are interested and passionate about it.

You already decided that this is the area of study that you want to make a career in.

You study hard and do your projects diligently because you understand your responsibility.

You discover that there are particular things in your area of study that you do easily and that you immensely like doing.

You know that if you study hard and follow all the instructions you will get good grades and marks in your tests and examinations.

And if you follow and attend all your classes, study well and keep your relationships with your friends, family, and teachers on the positive side and pass your examinations year after year then you get a graduation or a professional degree after say 3-5 years.

Exactly in the same way your work lottery is working for you in your first phase inside your personal boundary.

The only difference is that instead of studying and attending your classes like in the college you are here studying and working in your job or employment.

Your boss or your manager and the management and your clients and your customers are now your teachers and principals and administration and your examiners and your salary, paycheck or your commissions are now your marks, scores, or grades.

I call this period in your personal boundary as your School and College of Capitalism as shown in Figure - 2.

Any form of employment or self-employment is also just like a school and a college where instead of getting marks, scores, and grades you are getting money in the form of a salary or a commission.

You can regard your school of capitalism as purely a job or employment in a small or large organization and your college of capitalism as more of self-employment where you are your own boss and manage your work for your clients.

So it is in your school and college of capitalism where you decide how long you want to continue as you can pass out from your school and take admission in your college.

What I mean by this is that you can choose self-employment after being an employee in an organization.

In your self-employment or your college of capitalism, this is like a degree course for you that may not end after 3-5 years but may continue for your entire lifetime if you wish or choose to.

The point that you always need to keep in mind in this school or college of capitalism is that you have to always focus on the process and not on the score.

If you actually enjoy going through the process and keep your focus there then the quality and the amount of score will automatically follow for you.

So what do I mean here by the equation Process = Score in your school or college of capitalism?

Figure -3 explains this equation as a snapshot.

Process	Results/Scores
Your Individuality As Expressed By Your Passion & Talents In Your Job/Employment/ Self-Employment + Your Support System	Money In The Form Of Salary/Paycheck/ Commissions/ Invoice Payments

Yes, the process is your work, job, employment, or self-employment that you do with your individual passion, knowledge, or interest that you have along with the work that you can do as per your talents so that you enjoy that work and you find it easy to do it compared to others.

On top of that, you have a support system which I explained in detail in the last chapter which together is going to decide the result of your work in the form of money, salary, paycheck, or commission as your score.

You should not focus on your score or money in your employment as it is not going to help you.

If you only focus on the money then this can lead you to frustrations and unhappiness and jealousy but if you focus on the process of doing your work well and at the same time you enjoy this entire process because it is based upon your passions and talents then you are bound to get good results in the form of money.

Like in school or college you study well and hard and give your examinations to get good results and marks so similarly in your school or college of capitalism you work well and hard to get money in the form of a salary, paycheck or commission.

In your school or college of capitalism, however, you give your tests and examinations each day to your boss, employers, customers, and clients.

Yes, you have to pass with good results by giving your exams each day by understanding your work and working diligently at your job, employment or self-employment.

Only then you will be happy to get your money in the end.

So your money in the form of a salary, paycheck, or commissions is a by-product of the kind and quality of the work that you do in your employment or self-employment.

If you only focus on your money or salary or paycheck or commissions then they are not going to come to you and also will not expand or increase but if you wholeheartedly focus on your individual process of passions, interests, goals, knowledge, talents, skills, abilities and efforts along with maintaining and building your support system then these things are going to expand, improve, increase and become better with time.

And when this happens money will automatically come to you, follow you like a servant and like a pet dog.

This is true as money is a very good servant for you and is in no way a master of you.

There is, however, one thing that you need to be cautious about while seeking your work and employment.,

Never work for a company, employer, or a cheap client, who does not pay well as per the market norms and standards, who does not pay on time as agreed upon or who does not pay at all.

Yes, there are such cheap, untrustworthy, and dishonest companies and people in the market and you need to be careful and alert about them.

This does happen sometimes in a traditional job or employment but it more happens nowadays in the digital space especially in a freelance or contractual form of employment or any cheap online job.

But one thing you should keep in mind is that you will receive your scores, that is your money in the form of your salary, bonus or commissions always as per the kind, amount and quality of work that you do to create any kind of value for your employer, clients or customers in the market.

So your job is to always pay attention and keep your focus on the process as illustrated in Figure - 3.

This process is going to remain special to you because you will be here doing your work that you love or like doing and that you do this work easily and you enjoy doing this work, of course, helped and strengthened further with your support system.

Let's now look at some of the benefits of going through the process of work which is based upon your passions, interests, goals, knowledge, talents, skills, abilities, and your efforts along with your own support system.

1. You will be happy in your job, looking forward to your entire day when you get up from your sleep in the morning.

2. You will do more without feeling miserable, overburdened, or stressed.

3. Since you'll be happy working, the other areas of your life attached to your support system will also be happy and meaningful which in turn will make you more productive in your work. So, it is like a cycle as illustrated in Figure - 2.

4. Most important benefit that you are going to have is that you'll enjoy making money for yourself. The money that you will receive by following this process will give you immense joy and happiness.

So, this is your work lottery in the first phase of your personal boundary and I know you can win it by following the guidelines and the process flowchart which I have discussed with you.

Don't you think you are already rich in every way if you follow this process?

You should know that the majority of your waking hours out of the total 24 hours are spent on work.

So, if your waking hours are spent only by doing work based upon your passions, interests, goals, knowledge, talents, skills, abilities and you make your efforts in that direction don't you think you are rich as you are getting paid for going through this process.

Money is just a man-made resource that only has an exchange value for buying other goods and services.

It is nothing more than that.

But your time that you spend in your total waking hours in a day is an asset.

It is the most valuable asset that you have.

So if you can enjoy your time by working in a job, employment or self-employment and also get paid for doing so then I think you are rich.

And it does not cost you any money to get rich in this way.

As I have already discussed with you there are many types and forms of working.

You can work in a big traditional company or you can work in a small or a mid-sized private company, you can work in a big MNC or a corporate company, you can work in a government organization, you can work in an educational institution, you can work from your home, you can work online on the Internet, you can work for an employer or a company or you can work for your own self by getting your own clients, you can buy and sell by having your own customers, you can trade, you can provide teaching and consultancy and so on.

In whatever way and capacity you are working you are trading your manual efforts and time for money.

So a job, employment or self-employment of any form and type is a manual process of generating your income.

Therefore, make sure that you are enjoying and looking forward to this time in your each waking productive day.

You can continue to do this work that you enjoy for your entire lifetime if you wish to and you will never require retiring.

Just make sure that you save regularly the money that you make from this process.

This manual process of trading your time for money takes care of your two needs.

One is your basic and comfort need for money and the other is your random need for money..

The basic need of money fulfills all your basic needs like paying for your daily and monthly bills of all kinds which you know you have to pay or need to pay.

The random need for money fulfills all your sudden and unexpected needs or requirements like house repair, buying a house or a car, medical hospitalization, doctor's bill, education and training bills, etc. which are expenses that are not regular in nature but are expenses that you have to bear sometimes or unexpectedly.

Therefore you should save regularly in order to meet your random need for money.

There is nothing wrong at all by working for money in a job, employment or self employment as long as you are happy and enjoying it each day in your waking time and hours.

This can definitely make you rich because by working while enjoying it is as good as living a rich life.

This is your school and college of capitalism and you can continue this school and college life for as long as you want.

This also means that you can remain in your school or college of capitalism forever and there is no need for you to pass out or graduate from here.

You have won your work lottery and it is going to meet all your life's needs except for one thing very important.

Yes, there is only one thing that you will not get here.

And that is "Freedom".

You can get rich in your school or college of capitalism but you will not have freedom.

Now, what do I mean by freedom here?

Freedom here means getting money for yourself without having to work for it.

Although, even if you are happy and enjoying your work, still you need to labor, work and put in your efforts each day to get your money for your basic and random needs.

If you stop working at any point in time then your salary, paycheck, bonuses, invoice payments and commissions will also stop coming to you.

This is a big problem, isn't it? And it's scary!

Of course, there are paid leaves and vacations in a job package and you can also delegate most of your work which you do not like doing yourself to your other assistants and employees in your self-employment but what if you permanently decide not to work for money anymore, that you are tired and not motivated to work for money further, then what you do?

What do you do if you long for retirement from work with a pension so that all your life's needs are met without having to work daily?

The answer and solution to this problem are that then you must pass out and graduate from your school or college of capitalism as quickly as possible with a degree.

And that college degree is your own business start-up which I am going to discuss in detail in the next chapter.

Having your own business is the only means by which you get your money to meet your needs for freedom.

In your school or college of capitalism, that is in the first phase of your work lottery inside your personal boundary apart from serving your employer, clients, or customers to get your payments, salary, bonuses, or commissions to meet your basic and random needs you are also required to study, learn, plan, design and give time to set up your own business so that you get the money to meet your needs of freedom.

Therefore, while working in your school or college of capitalism you must store or save a portion of your payments, salary, bonus, or commissions as you will require this money later on to start your own business.

You can do a job or employment or even self-employment free of cost but you do require money to set up and start your own business.

So in other words the marks or grades that you get in your school or college of capitalism will help you tremendously to pass out or graduate and move on and take admission in your University Of Capitalism which is the second or the next phase of your work lottery inside your personal boundary.

So, do very well in your school or college of capitalism to get good marks so that you can use these marks or scores to set up your own business to graduate and get a degree.

If you follow this system and process diligently and with discipline then you will never require any kind of financial help or aid from your friends, family members, grant organizations, angel investors, venture capitalists, and other loan-giving institutions to start and set up your own business.

You will be able to generate your own funds for setting up and running your business without having to go through the complexities of asking for financial help from others.

While going through your process of working and simultaneously building your support system in your school or college of capitalism you need to find time to study, learn and gather all the resources to set up and start your own business.

The business should already be up and running and generating passive income for you in your school or college of capitalism itself so that you can then take admission to your university of capitalism.

This business that you start in your school or college of capitalism should be generating enough income and profits for you that it can take care of you, it makes you secure so much that you do not have to return to the job market again for seeking employment of any kind.

You need to take care that your business should be profitable enough and financially stable that it makes you financially free and wealthy.

Wealth or being wealthy here means that your business generates enough income regularly and consistently so that you can meet your basic and random needs of money without having to work for it daily.

In other words, your income is more than your expenses without having to work for it.

When this happens with your business in your school or college of capitalism over a while then you should know and recognize that your college has awarded you with your graduation degree and that you are now qualified to enter and take admission in your university of capitalism to scale up, expand, and to grow your startup business further.

So, what is this business that I am talking about that provides you with an automated source of income?

What does it contain and entail?

How does it look like in your work lottery?

What are its parts and components, how is it structured?

What is its importance, functions and purpose in your work lottery and what qualifies something to be called a business?

I will be answering and discussing everything about a business and much more in the very next chapter.

So continue reading!.

CHAPTER 6
SYSTEMS AND AUTOMATION
- YOUR BUSINESS!

Playing And Winning Your Work Lottery By Running Your Own Business
As An Entrepreneur And As Business Owner And Your Results And
Scores To Earn Your University Degree By Successfully And
Profitably Running A Financially Stable Business!

We have reached a point now where there is a transition from an employee to an entrepreneur or a business owner happening in your work lottery inside your personal boundary.

This is also the second phase of your work lottery as illustrated in the process flowchart of Figure - 2.

Again, as I said before, there is nothing wrong at all to be an employee or a self- employee working in a job or working for your own self.

It does take care of your basic and random needs for money and life can be good, smooth, and happy along with the help of your support system here.

After all, you are working based upon your passions, interests, knowledge, goals, talents, skills, abilities, and efforts in getting paid at the end for all your hard work.

As long as there is joy, flow, and money in the work that you do you can continue to do so forever for your entire lifetime and keep on saving your money in the process as well.

But as I have pointed out before that there is one big drawback if you continue to remain in your school or college of capitalism and never pass out or graduate from there.

You are not going to get freedom from your work that you love and enjoy doing.

You will have no choice but to keep on working so that you keep on getting a steady paycheck or payments or commissions.

You cannot retire in the real sense of the word because if you stop working your money also stops coming in no matter how much you love and enjoy working.

Investing your saved money in mutual funds, stock markets, and other financial markets can be far more risky and unpredictable and they are not known to provide a source of stable and dependable income once you retire or stop working.

Buying pension schemes from the market also is not a very attractive proposition as the income through such market pensions is too low to live a comfortable retired life.

Investing money in bank fixed deposits can help you in the short term but may not carry you comfortably in the future long term as the bank interest rates keep on falling steadily after each financial year.

You might feel sick and tired working hard at some point in time and you may feel like doing something else or take a rest for which you do not want to actively work anymore for money.

Another big disadvantage of continuing to keep on working for money by remaining in your school or college of capitalism forever is that you never know when you can be out of work unexpectedly or suddenly.

It could be just that the company or business or employer or client that you work for doesn't need your services anymore.

Remember that if you are working for a company or a business or a client you are a rented asset for them.

Yes, you are rented the moment you are hired and you need to be consistently profitable for them.

So, there is no permanent employment as such nowadays and there is no job security until and unless you are employed properly in the government or some ministry where at least the job is secure and you are also going to get a pension for life once you retire from their working.

But in any private or corporate business, your job is not at all secured and you may lose your job anytime due to any reason.

It can be due to a reengineering in your department or company or it can be due to a layoff or it can be just that your boss or client does not like your services anymore or it can be any other business or personal reasons.

There is always a risk.

On top of that you now have long working hours, you have a 24/7 work environment where you may also be required to work at odd hours like night shifts, you may have to do multitasking jobs or you may have jobs in a high-pressure environment doing complicated tasks.

Then there is office politics and not getting good performance appraisals and increments and promotions.

All these things are serious demotivators towards healthy work output and productivity and at some point in time, you may feel that you are being exploited.

There can be frustration and anger and you may start thinking and wondering what you are actually working for after all without having any respite or escape from the daily grind.

A job can shut your creativity and you may not be able to see a good realistic future for yourself.

Even if you are self-employed as an independent contractor or working as a freelancer from home there is a problem.

You may not always get a stable, regular, or ongoing project to work upon for a long period.

You can frequently find yourself going out of work and therefore out of money and your income.

What do you do when all these things happen?

You again look for a job change or look for new work by searching and applying for various suitable jobs.

That is you again start buying your lottery tickets from the market to play and try to win your work lottery.

This is what happens or the chances are that it happens if you continue to stay in your school or college of capitalism forever without passing out or graduating from there.

It is a cycle and a process that you keep on repeating to find a happy and good future like a mirage.

Because if you are working for money in a business or a company or for an employer or a client you are actually a servant of them dictated by their rules, whims, and wishes no matter how much you like, love, and enjoy your work.

Although, you will still win your work lottery by remaining in your school or college of capitalism but that is a temporary solution.

Don't you think that instead of just working as a servant at somebody else's house it is far more sensible, wise, practical, and beneficial to build and own your own house?

You should have a permanent solution to your work and money problems and that is you must pass out and graduate and earn a professional degree from your school or college of capitalism by setting up, owning, and starting your own business and then take admission in your university of capitalism to grow and scale up your business further.

Let me give you an example to illustrate what I actually mean by a business that you earn as a professional degree to pass out or graduate from your school or college of capitalism.

Suppose there is a shop located in a market which has some goods and services that it sells to customers.

If you are working in this shop in any role or capacity then it is a job or employment that you do for a salary which is paid to you by the shopkeeper.

If you are the shopkeeper yourself and you own this shop but you go to your shop daily and sit there looking after the day to day activities of the shop and also service and cater to the customers who visit your shop on a daily basis then it is self-employment for you where it is your own job that you do for yourself.

This is still not a business for you as you are working in your own job.

But if you own this shop and you are not physically present in your shop on a daily basis nor you look after the daily activities of the shop all the while you collect the money which the shop makes from its sales and profits then it is a business for you.

Your physical presence and time are not required in your shop but you are still getting the money from the shop sitting at home doing absolutely nothing to run the day-to-day profit activities of the shop as there are hired employees who do that for you.

Similarly, if you are a professional doctor working in a hospital then that is a job for you.

But if you own your own clinic where you are giving medical service to your patients then it is a job that you own where you are self-employed.

Whereas, if you are a doctor who builds and owns a running hospital where other doctors are working and you are sitting at home to collect the monthly profits made by that hospital then that becomes your business.

The hospital that you own becomes a money-making machine for you where you need not work.

Your endeavor in your school or college of capitalism should be to build your own shop or hospital after working as a professional in a shop or a hospital.

That is your college degree and that degree signifies Systems and Automation.

The business truly means automation.

Automation of work and automation of your income generation.

Of course, there is an initial money investment and efforts required to set-up and start your own business and you need to constantly work on your business to see that this automated machine is running and functioning well and smoothly.

A job is a manual process of generating income, revenue, and money but a business is an automated process and system of generating income, revenue, or money.

A business can be an extension of the job that you already do.

That means you can build and own a business directly based upon your experience, field, and area of work that you do in a job, or you can build and own a business totally unrelated to your experience or career field in your employment or job.

For example, you may be an I.T. professional working in a corporate organization and so you may want to build and own a business that is related to the I.T. industry like owning and running a blog or a website that solves computer hardware and software problems of customers.

But being an I.T. professional you may build and own a totally different kind of business that is totally unrelated to the IT industry like real estate.

The point is that the business you set-up, start, build and grow should also be based upon your individual process of passion, knowledge, interest, goals, talents, skills, abilities, and efforts as discussed in Chapter - 3.

So you would essentially be needing three main components of your work lottery in your personal boundary in order to activate this component of business or systems and automation.

These three components are the ones that we have already discussed and are an essential requirement as a process outflow for your business as illustrated in Figure - 2.

They are -

1. Your passions, knowledge, interests, goals, talents, skills, abilities, and efforts.

2. The support system that you build and maintain in your school or college of capitalism.

3. Your results and scores or the money that you receive, save and store in your school or college of capitalism in order to start your own business.

As in Figure - 2 you can see that the systems and automation component which is nothing else but your business is an extension of the process flowchart of the above three components.

Like in your school or college of capitalism you should take up work or job based upon your passions, interests, knowledge, goals, talents, skills, abilities and efforts similarly it is very important that you set-up and start your own business for which you have a passion for, the subjects or topics or field that you are always interested in and you should have good or expert knowledge about the business that you enter into.

In your school or college of capitalism, it becomes your duty to not only work for your money but also study and learn everything that you need to know about the business that you are going to start.

Here your support system will come to your help like your teachers, mentors, business coaches, your professional contacts and network, etc...

Also, you should start only that business where you think you have the talent, skill, and ability to do so.

So to set up and start your own business is just like any other work that you were already doing in your school or college of capitalism to earn an income but the only biggest difference is that of automation.

Now, you will be creating and building your own system and a machine that is automated and runs by its own self.

You will, of course, need the money to invest in building this machine for yourself which you earn, save and store in your school or college of capitalism.

Let's now look inside this business machine. What does it look like? What are the parts of this business system, process, or machine that needs to be automated?

Figure - 4 illustrates this process or system or machine which is the detailed and enlarged version of the systems and automation component of Figure - 2.

This is the exact blueprint of your business which can be applied to any kind or type of business that you would want to set up and start from scratch.

So let me now dive into the detailed explanation of each nut and bolt of this business blueprint.

1. What Do Your Customers Want In The Market -

Before setting up this system you need to reach up to the market again to find out what your customers really want?

What is that product or service that you would supply or sell to your market for which there is an unmet need?

To find that out you can do market research and customer surveys to select your niche or to find out the need in the market that you would like to meet and solve.

Please keep in mind that now your market is represented by your customers and not by your employer, boss, or management.

Instead of the resource market, it is now the product market.

In your job, the market is a resource market where you are the resource for a business but when you're starting your own business the market becomes a product market where you are going to create and sell products or services to your customers.

One trick that you can follow to find the market or customer need for your products and services is to create a "Customer Avatar".

A customer avatar is like the personality of your customer. How does your customer look like, what is the age group, gender, and income level that you are targeting?

What are your customer's deep-rooted problems that need to be solved?

So, the trick here is to imagine your own self as the biggest customer for your own business and then try to design and provide a solution, help, plan, benefit, and answers in the form of your products and services.

2. Product Or Value Creation To Serve And Solve –

After finding out about what your customers or the market really want, you start creating and designing your own products or services to meet that market demand.

This is known as value creation in the form of products and services in your business.

The product or service that you create is going to be the value that you give to your customers or the market.

The value here means what is the solution that you are providing to your customer's problems, or the benefit or help that you are providing to your customers in the market that you found out from your market research or customer survey.

3. Marketing And Sales -

It is your job in your business to get customers and keep them as your customers for the products and services that you create.

You need to go through proper marketing funnels to put your products and services in front of your customers.

In short, you need to be a salesman or a supplier of your products and services as value.

4. Generate Income, Profits, And Cash Flow -

It is your responsibility to collect payments from your customers for the products and services that you sell to them.

In other words, you should design all the ways, means, and methods to receive your income from the sales that you do to your customers in your business.

5. Automation Of The Processes, Procedures, And Systems To Print Your Own Money-

Since business is automation, you need to automate this process or parts of the system that I just discussed from steps 1 to 4 above.

This is the complete structure of a true business. Any business that you start from scratch has to follow these 5 parts or components.

Your business is supposed to work like a bank where ultimately you are able to print your own money instead of you working hard for money like in a job.

A business that you create and build has to be an asset for you where it puts money in your pocket without you having to work for it or be physically present for its day-to-day activities.

This is the second phase of your work lottery and it takes you to your University of Capitalism.

In your University of Capitalism, you are supposed to grow, expand and scale up this business further.

This is where you are going to get your freedom money, a type of money for which you do not need to labor day in and day out.

Freedom money can give you freedom from the job market and freedom from working for money to get your basic and random needs met.

You will never be required to do a job again for someone else.

You become an entrepreneur who creates profitable businesses in your university of capitalism and becomes a complete capitalist printing your own money to invest or buy other assets, of course, by taking the help of your support system.

Your support system will now consist of people like your business coaches, business teachers, employees, and other business team members.

Below is a list of benefits or privileges that you will have once you become a capitalist.

1. You will have the freedom to choose when, what and how to work.

2. Your business is going to give you the time, money, and freedom to write books if you want to be based upon your knowledge and experience and earn royalty income.

3. Your business is going to give you the money and the time to learn, gain knowledge, and get trained to buy real estate and properties and earn rental income.

4. Your business is going to give you the money and time to learn and get trained about the stock market and invest in other businesses and become a shareholder of other companies and businesses.

5. Your business is going to give you the money, knowledge and experience to buy other businesses that you might be interested in running.

Not everybody would like to take admission in this university of capitalism and they would prefer to remain in their school or college of capitalism and that is absolutely fine.

So, this is the complete process flow chart of your work lottery which everyone can win.

In the next to last chapter, I am going to summarize this work lottery as a whole and let you know the overall benefits of following it.

So read on!

CHAPTER 7
CONCLUSION

Your Work Lottery For Your Dream Job, Promotions And Career Growth!

I hope by now you have an understanding of how you can buy and win your work lottery, what it looks like, what it contains, and how it works.

To conclude, let me summarize this entire work lottery for you as listed below and also explain to you the overall purpose and benefits of it.

a) Market (Demand)

b) Personal Boundary (Supply)

c) Passions, Interests, Knowledge, Goals (Energy)

d) Talents, Skills, Abilities, Efforts (Tools)

e) Support System (Team, Family, Friends, Personal and Professional Helpers)

f) School Of Capitalism (Job, Employment)

g) College Of Capitalism (Freelancer, Trader, Self-Employment)

h) University Of Capitalism (Systems And Automation - Business)

i) Results And Scores (Salary, Commissions, Sales/Business Income,

Profits)

So, we have the market which is the demand for work, products, and services as represented by your boss, manager, employer, company, business, clients, and customers.

You, working as per your passions, interests, knowledge, goals, talents, skills, abilities, and efforts inside your personal boundary is the supplier of that work or the need for products and services in the market.

You, as a supplier inside your personal boundary, fulfills that need or demand of the market with the help of your support system either through a job, employment, self-employment, trading, or through a business in primarily two phases.

The first phase is your School Of Capitalism where you are basically an employee of an organization doing a job inside your personal boundary and generating your results and scores in the form of a salary or a paycheck.

The first phase is also your College Of Capitalism where you are basically a freelancer, trader or a self-employed independent contractor may be working remote, virtual or from your home inside your personal boundary and setting up and building a start-up business while generating your results and scores in the form of invoice payments, commissions, sales/business income.

The second phase is your University Of Capitalism where you are a full-fledged entrepreneur and a business owner growing and expanding your start-up business further and generating your results and scores only by printing your own money by automated selling machines, profits, and other business revenues.

The Ultimate Benefits And The Purpose Served By Your Work Lottery

Let me at the end analyze a few benefits and the purpose served once you have activated your work lottery in your life and career.

1. Firstly, this work lottery is going to give you promotions and growth in your career.

   If you are not getting promotions in your job and career then you can actually self-promote yourself by following your work lottery.

   You can start by doing a traditional job in an organization in your school of capitalism from where you can pass out and take admission in your college of capitalism and become an independent self-employee.

   It is easier to create your own start-up business in your college of capitalism as there are far more flexibility and freedom in your working lifestyle here than in your school of capitalism.

   From there on you can graduate from your college of capitalism and take admission in your university of capitalism where you can become a complete entrepreneur and a business owner.

2. Your work lottery will ensure that you get your most suitable dream job.

3. By going through the various stages of your work lottery you will get an opportunity to do both a job and a business at the same time.

4. Provides you with an opportunity to transition from an employee to an entrepreneur and increase your earnings with time.

5. You will not need financial help from others to fund your start-up business as you can self-finance your business from earning and storing your money by doing a job.

6. You will find work satisfaction and happiness in your job or business as this work lottery ensures that you take up work as per your passions, interests, knowledge, goals, talents, skills, abilities, and efforts.

7. Your support system will keep on updating and enhancing your skills, knowledge, and other work-related resources both in your employment and in your business.

8. Your support system will ensure that you are happy in your personal and social life as well.

9. You can become a capitalist where you can print your own money legally like a bank which can further help you to buy and invest in other money-making assets.

So you see that this lottery ticket is actually a roadmap for you to become rich and wealthy by taking the route of an employee to a self-employee to an entrepreneur and ultimately becoming a capitalist.

I hope you are going to use this guideline and benefit from it by staying in this course and in this journey of health, wealth, happiness and prosperity.

Thank you for reading my book.

Enjoy and have fun!

I wish you the best.

This is your friend Subho Dutta from Capitalist College.

ABOUT THE AUTHOR

I am Subho Dutta. I work online and have embraced the Internet lifestyle. I like writing and love creating digital content where I express my thoughts, feelings, views, opinions, my existing knowledge, experience and my first-hand search findings that I have acquired over time after years and years of working hard in many private companies and in the corporate world.

I am the creator of Capitalist College which is an institution with the sole purpose to help and give solutions to all the working professionals and lifelong student community in the areas that I know about like jobs, career and employment, employer and employee relationship, boss, management and leadership, entrepreneurship and capitalism, business, sales and sources of income, money and how it works, getting rich, retirement and lifestyle solutions and many other such topics. It is my aim and my endeavor here to make education and career and learning and working fun, interesting, exciting, inspiring and motivating which have been traditionally considered to be boring.

"How To Win A Lottery By Just Doing A Job" is meant to serve this purpose for success, growth and direction in today's capitalist economy and society.

You can also visit my blog -
https://capitalistcollege.blogspot.com
and like and follow my Facebook page -
https://www.facebook.com/CapitalistCollege where I keep on

updating with articles and other resources to help you succeed in your job, career, business, money, and retirement goals.

I also want you to refer and share my blog and my Facebook page with your friends and family members so that more and more people become aware of the various solutions that are available to their work and money problems and are able to benefit and take advantage of them as working professionals and as lifelong students to realize their job, career and business dreams and ambitions.